PECULIAR DOG AWARDS

Written by Annabel Griffin   Illustrated by Marina Halak

Copyright © 2024 Hungry Tomato Ltd

First published in 2024 by Hungry Tomato Ltd
F15, Old Bakery Studios, Blewetts Wharf, Malpas Road, Truro, Cornwall,
TR1 1QH, UK.

No part of this publication may be reproduced, stored in a retrieval system, or transmitted in any form or by any means, electronic, mechanical, photocopying, recording, or otherwise, without prior written permission of the copyright owner.

A CIP catalogue record for this book is available from the British Library.

ISBN 9781916598737

Printed in China

Discover more at
www.hungrytomato.com

CONTENTS

The World of Dogs	4
Breed Groups	6
Peculiar Dog Awards	8
Biggest and Smallest	9
Iconic Noses	10
Longest and Lowest	12
Fluffiest Coats	14
Longest Coats	16
Funniest Hair	18
Spottiest Dog	20
Historic Breeds	22
What's That Dog?	24
Spot the Dog	26
Training and Rewards	28
Glossary	30
Index	31

Words in **BOLD** can be found in the glossary.

THE WORLD OF DOGS

Get ready to explore the wonderful world of peculiar dogs! From the hairiest dogs to the longest, there are so many different types of lovable dogs to discover.

This breed is super old!

WHERE DO DOGS COME FROM?

Believe it or not, all dogs are **descendants** of ancient wolves. The details of how and when wolves became dogs are still quite foggy, but it likely started when humans began to **domesticate** and train wolves, at least 14,000 years ago. Today, dogs can be found all over the world.

Big and small, they've got it all!

WHAT IS A BREED?

A breed is a particular group of dogs that all share the same (or very similar) appearance and **characteristics**, making them easy to identify. There are hundreds of different breeds, and they can vary wildly in size, shape, hairiness, and personality.

Not all dogs belong to a specific breed. Some dogs, known as mutts or mongrels, are a mixture of lots of different breeds. They can make fantastic pets, and can often be found looking for a loving home at rescue or **rehoming shelters.**

GETTING A DOG?

Maybe you already have a dog in your family, or maybe you'd like to in the future. Owning a dog can be fun and rewarding, but it's also a big responsibility. Some dogs need a lot of space, time and attention. Before buying or **adopting** a dog, you should always carefully research their breed and think about whether you are able to give them everything they need to be happy.

Not all dogs can be as talented as this one!

BREED GROUPS

Dog breeds are often arranged into seven different groups, that are loosely based on the jobs that they were originally bred to do.

SPORTING GROUP

Also known as gundogs, these dogs were originally bred to help hunters retrieve birds.

NON-SPORTING GROUP

This is the group for dogs that don't fit into any of the other groups, so they are quite a mixed bunch!

TERRIER GROUP

This group were originally bred to hunt burrowing animals, such as rats, rabbits, foxes, and badgers. Most of them have "terrier" as part of their name.

WORKING GROUP

Dogs in this group were originally bred to perform practical tasks, such as pulling sleds and carts. They were also often used as watchdogs. They are usually large dogs.

SIGHTHOUNDS
These dogs are usually long, lean and very fast.

SCENT HOUNDS
These dogs have droopy ears and powerful noses.

HOUND GROUP

Hounds were bred for their sense of smell or sight, and were usually used for hunting. They can be split into two sub-groups: sighthounds and scent hounds.

HERDING GROUP

This group includes dogs that were bred to work on farms; herding and guarding livestock, such as sheep and cows.

TOY GROUP

Tiny breeds that are small enough to sit in your lap fall into this group. They are bred mostly as pets and companions.

PECULIAR DOG AWARDS

Welcome to the Peculiar Dog Awards! We're celebrating dogs who dare to be different. From the biggest to the smallest, the fluffiest to the spottiest, these dogs all have something that makes them stand out from the crowd. Dotty dalmatians, popular poodles, and the rare yodelling New Guinea singing dog, all feature on the list of amazing award winners. Which dog would you give the award for funniest hairdo?

BIGGEST AND SMALLEST   9

Irish Wolfhound

The award for the tallest dog goes to the Irish wolfhound. This shaggy dog can reach a whopping 86cm in height and weighs up to 68kg. They are gentle giants who love spending time with their humans.

Shaggy coat
Hairy muzzle
Big, strong body
Needs a lot of food

ORIGIN: Ireland
COAT: Medium-length, **wiry**
PERSONALITY: Patient and easy-going

INTELLIGENCE
ENERGY LEVEL
TRAINABILITY

Chihuahua

The Chihuahua is the smallest dog in the world, weighing no more than 3kg and as little as 13cm tall. These dogs have a BIG PERSONALITY in a pocket-sized body!

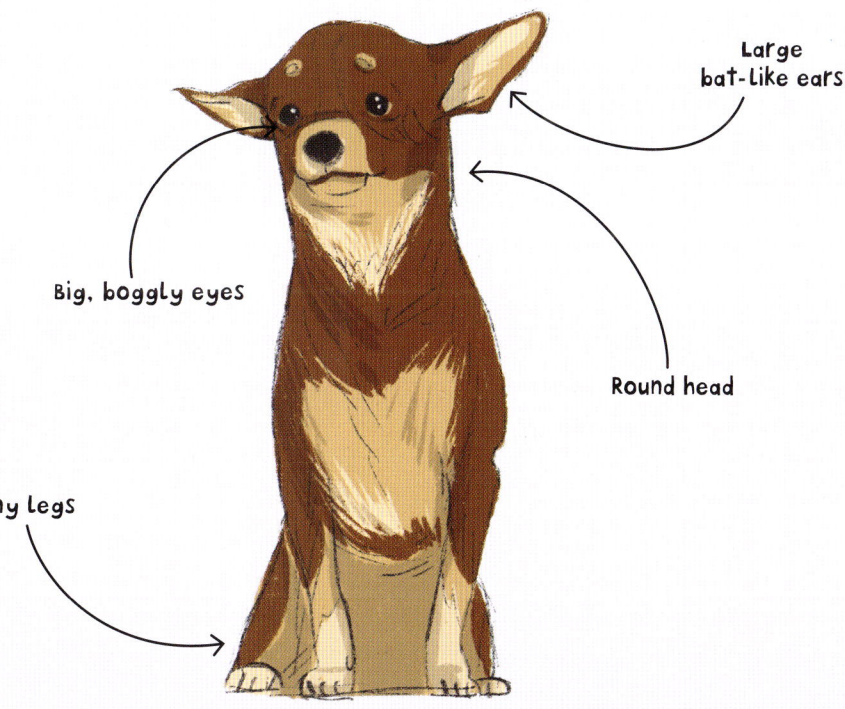

Large bat-like ears
Big, boggly eyes
Round head
Tiny legs

ORIGIN: Mexico
COAT: Short or medium-length, smooth
PERSONALITY: Alert and sassy

INTELLIGENCE
ENERGY LEVEL
TRAINABILITY

10 ICONIC NOSES

Bulldog

Bulldogs are well known for their short, upturned noses. This famous breed are known for being brave and friendly, but they can also be quite stubborn.

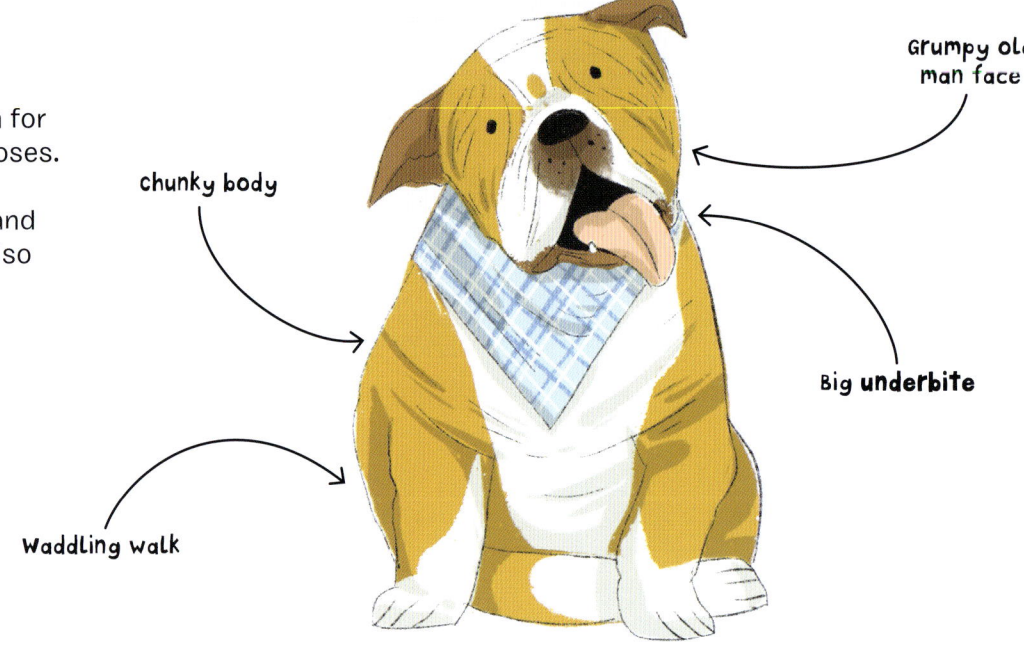

- Grumpy old man face
- chunky body
- Big underbite
- Waddling walk

ORIGIN: United Kingdom
COAT: Short, smooth
PERSONALITY: Sweet and goofy

INTELLIGENCE ●●○○○
ENERGY LEVEL ●●●○○
TRAINABILITY ●●●●○

Affenpinscher

Affenpinschers have monkey-like looks, with a flat face and tiny nose with wide nostrils. These little dogs are confident, curious and funny.

- Round, hairy face
- Upright tail
- Tiny nose with wide nostrils
- Black, wiry coat

ORIGIN: Germany
COAT: Medium-length, wiry
PERSONALITY: Mischievous and stubborn

INTELLIGENCE ●●●●○
ENERGY LEVEL ●●●○○
TRAINABILITY ●●●●○

ICONIC NOSES 11

Bull Terrier

Bull terriers are famous for their long "egg heads", and sloping noses. They are playful and clownish characters with bundles of confidence.

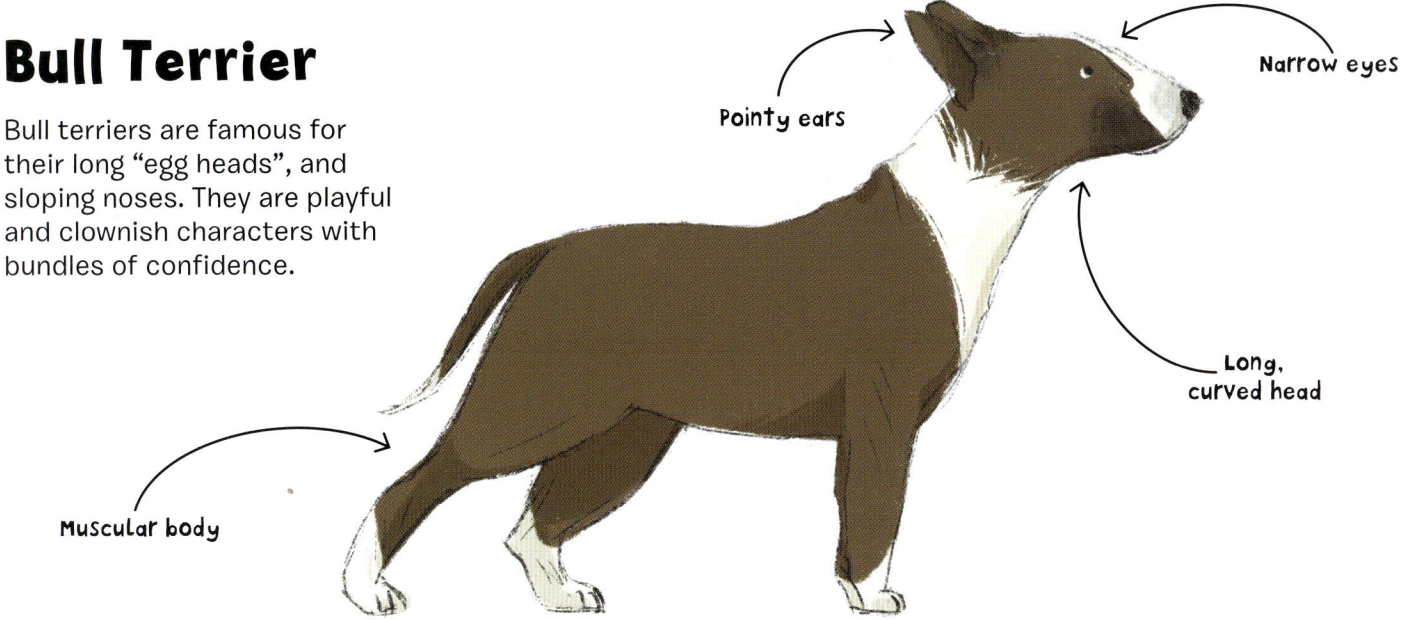

Pointy ears
Narrow eyes
Long, curved head
Muscular body

ORIGIN: United Kingdom
COAT: Short, smooth
PERSONALITY: Fun and feisty

INTELLIGENCE
ENERGY LEVEL
TRAINABILITY

Borzoi

The winner of the longest nose award has to go to the borzoi. Their proud, regal look matches their history, as they were originally bred to hunt wolves for Russian **tsars** and nobles.

Why the long face?
Thick fur on neck
Long and lanky body
Loves to run

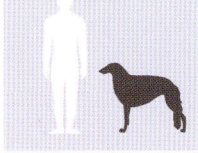

ORIGIN: Russia
COAT: Medium-length, wavy, silky
PERSONALITY: Calm and graceful

INTELLIGENCE
ENERGY LEVEL
TRAINABILITY

LONGEST AND LOWEST

Dachshund

Affectionately known as "sausage dogs", dachshunds are famous for their long bodies and little legs. They are a much-loved breed with a big personality. They are alert and loud, and make good little watchdogs.

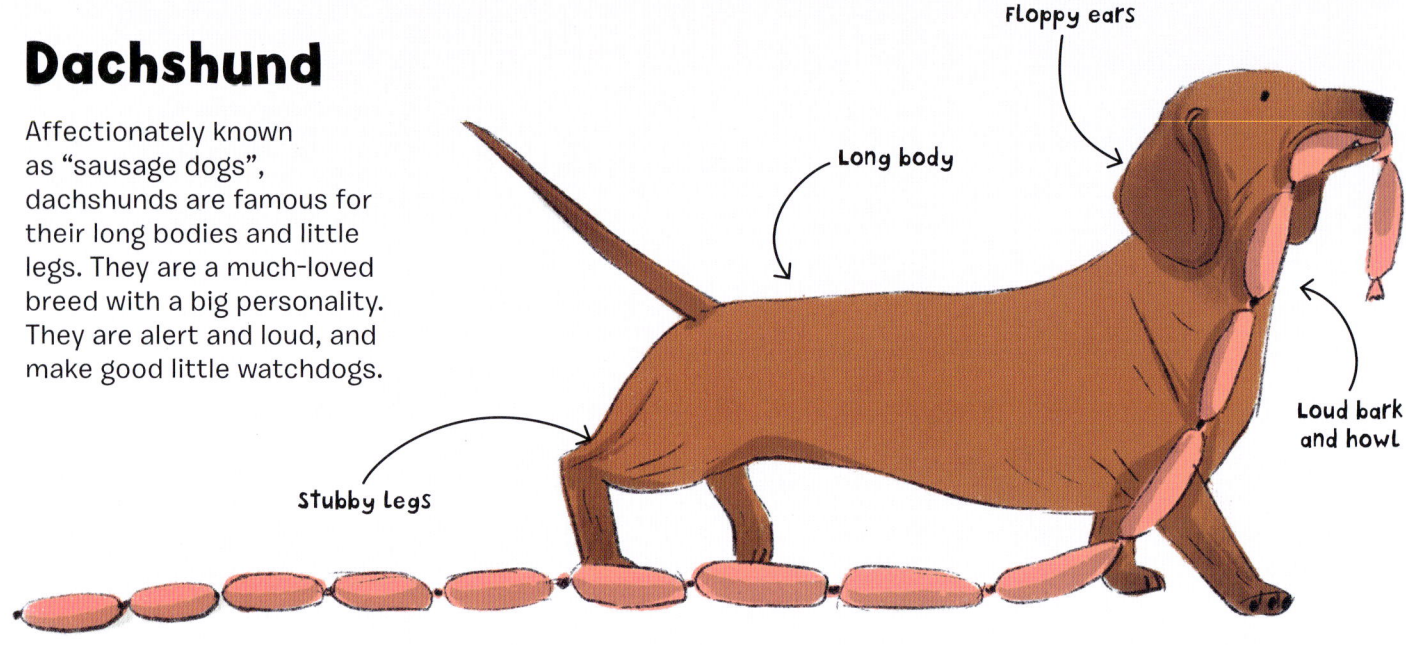

- Floppy ears
- Long body
- Loud bark and howl
- Stubby legs

ORIGIN: Germany

COAT: Short, smooth/short, wiry/long, silky

PERSONALITY: Lovable but stubborn

INTELLIGENCE	
ENERGY LEVEL	
TRAINABILITY	

- Smooth-haired dachshund
- Long-haired dachshund
- Wire-haired dachshund

LONGEST AND LOWEST 13

Dandie Dinmont Terrier

These funny-looking little dogs have one of the lowest tummies around! They were bred to fit down badger **burrows**, which helps to explain their long and low shape!

Fabulous hairdo!

Belly almost on the floor

Large, dark eyes

ORIGIN: United Kingdom
COAT: Medium, thick
PERSONALITY: Charming and social

INTELLIGENCE
ENERGY LEVEL
TRAINABILITY

Skye Terrier

Skye terriers have a big body on little legs. They are very loyal, brave and affectionate companions.

Eyes somewhere under the curtain of hair

Feathery legs

Looks like a walking broom

ORIGIN: United Kingdom
COAT: Long, silky
PERSONALITY: Loving and confident

INTELLIGENCE
ENERGY LEVEL
TRAINABILITY

14 FLUFFIEST COATS

Bichon Frisé

These fluffy little dogs have a personality as cuddly as their looks. They require a lot of grooming to get them looking their best, puffiest self.

often given a round haircut

Black nose

Thick, white, curly coat

ORIGIN: The Canary Islands (Spain)
COAT: Medium-length, curly
PERSONALITY: Confident and affectionate

INTELLIGENCE
ENERGY LEVEL
TRAINABILITY

Keeshond

These gorgeous fluffy dogs were first used as watch dogs on barge boats along the canals of the Netherlands. They are smart and easy to train.

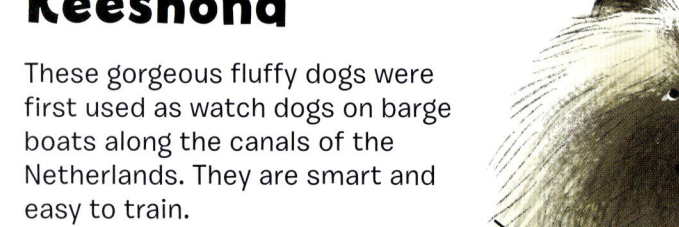

Bushy tail

Thick, puffy mane

Black, grey and cream markings

ORIGIN: The Netherlands
COAT: Long, very thick
PERSONALITY: Friendly and inquisitive

INTELLIGENCE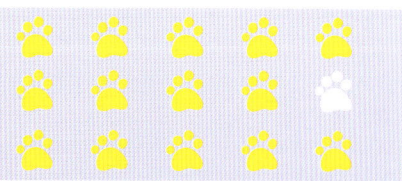
ENERGY LEVEL
TRAINABILITY

FLUFFIEST COATS 15

Pekingese

The Pekingese started off as a royal **lapdog** in China. It was only allowed to be owned by members of the Imperial Palace. They can be snooty with strangers, but are loving towards their owners.

Flat face

Fuzzy everywhere!

Probably has legs somewhere under all that fur!

ORIGIN: China
COAT: Long, very thick
PERSONALITY: Charming and relaxed

INTELLIGENCE	🐾🐾
ENERGY LEVEL	🐾🐾🐾
TRAINABILITY	🐾🐾🐾

Chow Chow

Despite their fluffy appearance, chow chows aren't known for being the friendliest dogs. Though they can form close bonds with their owners, they aren't big cuddlers. They are usually quiet and suspicious of strangers.

A lion in disguise?

Thick, fleecy coat

Scowling face

ORIGIN: China
COAT: Medium-length, very thick
PERSONALITY: Calm and independent

INTELLIGENCE	🐾🐾🐾
ENERGY LEVEL	🐾🐾🐾
TRAINABILITY	🐾🐾🐾

16 LONGEST COATS

Afghan Hound

This glamorous, ancient sighthound has an extra-long, silky coat, which would have originally protected them from extreme weather conditions in the mountains of Afghanistan.

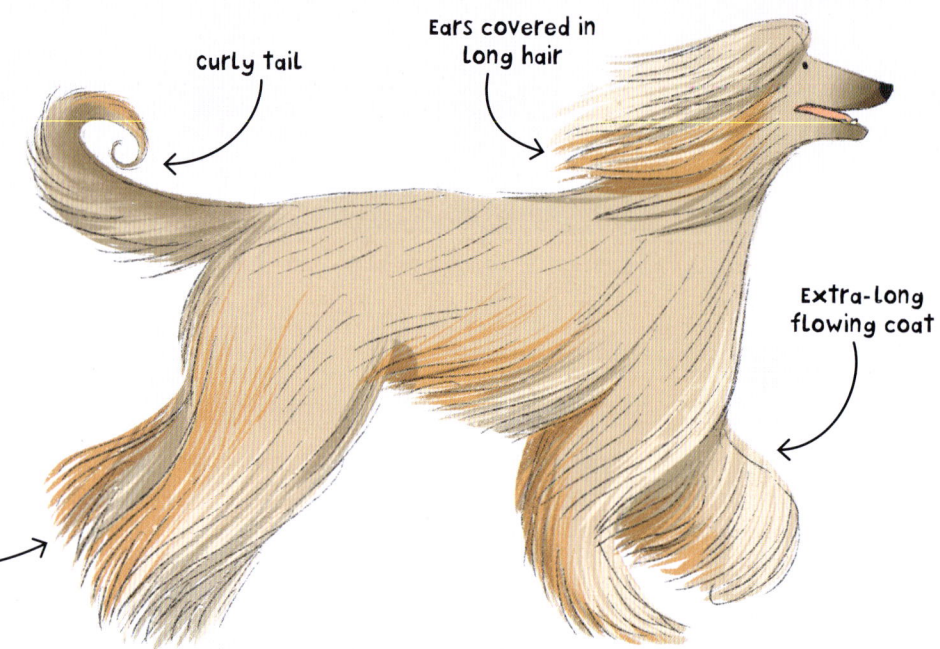

- curly tail
- Ears covered in long hair
- Extra-long flowing coat
- Doesn't shed much hair

ORIGIN: Afghanistan
COAT: Long, silky
PERSONALITY: Independent and gentle

INTELLIGENCE
ENERGY LEVEL
TRAINABILITY

Komondor

These Hungarian sheepdogs have one of the longest and most unusual coats around. Covered from head to toe in long, tasselled cords, these dogs stand out!

- Eyes and ears somewhere under all the hair!
- Loves the outdoors
- Long, heavy, white coats

ORIGIN: Hungary
COAT: Long, **corded**
PERSONALITY: Brave and affectionate

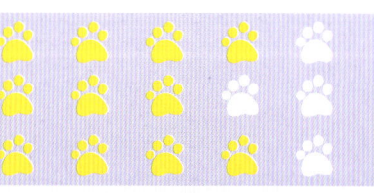

INTELLIGENCE
ENERGY LEVEL
TRAINABILITY

LONGEST COATS 17

Yorkshire Terrier

You wouldn't think it from their beauty-pageant looks, but these little dogs were originally bred to catch rats in mills and mines of Northern England. They are elegant but scrappy little dogs, with big personalities.

Long beard blends in with the rest of coat

Yappy bark

Silky coat, can be long enough to trail on the floor

ORIGIN: United Kingdom
COAT: Long, silky
PERSONALITY: Confident and friendly

INTELLIGENCE
ENERGY LEVEL
TRAINABILITY

Bearded Collie

The bearded collie's long, shaggy coat is perfect for working outdoors in all weather. These friendly, tireless, working sheepdogs can also make loving pets.

Large, black nose

Long, thick and silky coat

Long moustache

ORIGIN: United Kingdom
COAT: Long, silky, thick
PERSONALITY: Playful and affectionate

INTELLIGENCE
ENERGY LEVEL
TRAINABILITY

18 | FUNNIEST HAIR

Bedlington Terrier

These fluffy terriers look like little lambs. Their traditional **"show clip"** gives them an unusual curved head shape. They are speedy, athletic and caring dogs, with a big bark.

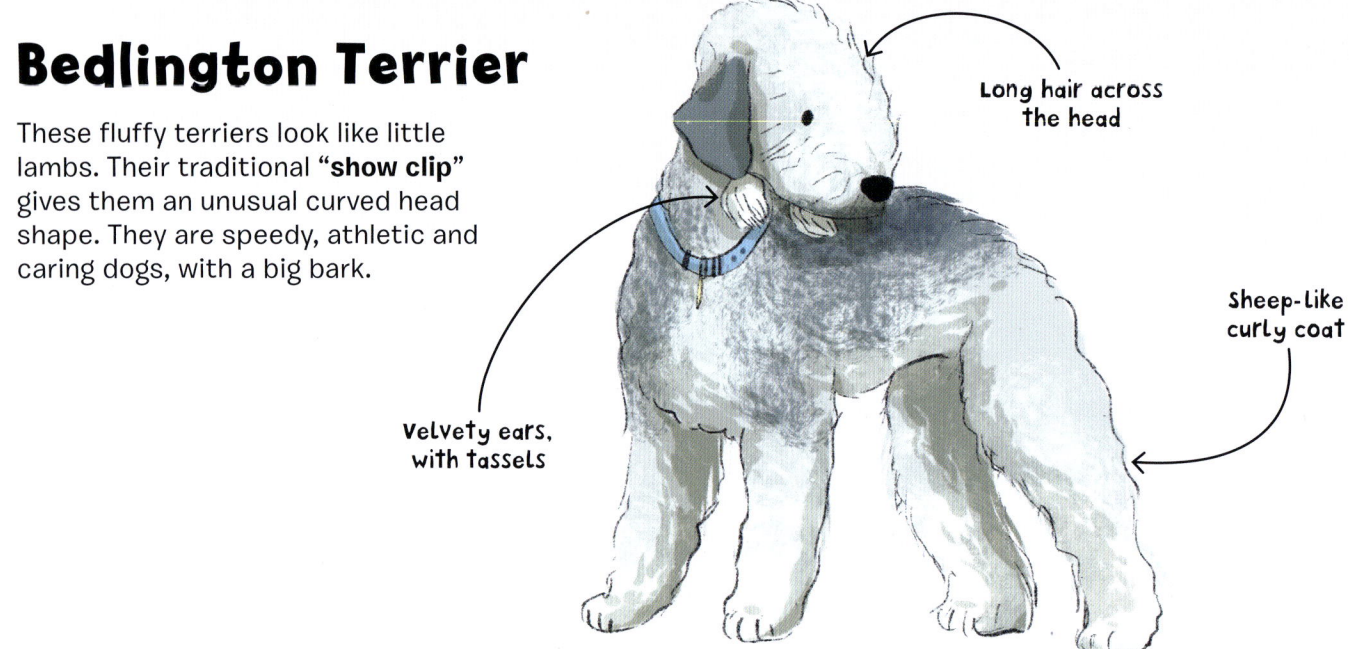

Long hair across the head

Sheep-like curly coat

Velvety ears, with tassels

ORIGIN: United Kingdom
COAT: Medium-length, curly
PERSONALITY: Cheerful and loyal

INTELLIGENCE 🐾🐾🐾
ENERGY LEVEL 🐾🐾🐾🐾
TRAINABILITY 🐾🐾🐾

Chinese Crested

This dog's odd looks may not be everyone's cup of tea, but they make lively and affectionate lapdogs. They often need to wear a jumper to keep warm in the winter, and have to avoid the hot sun in the summer, as their skin burns easily.

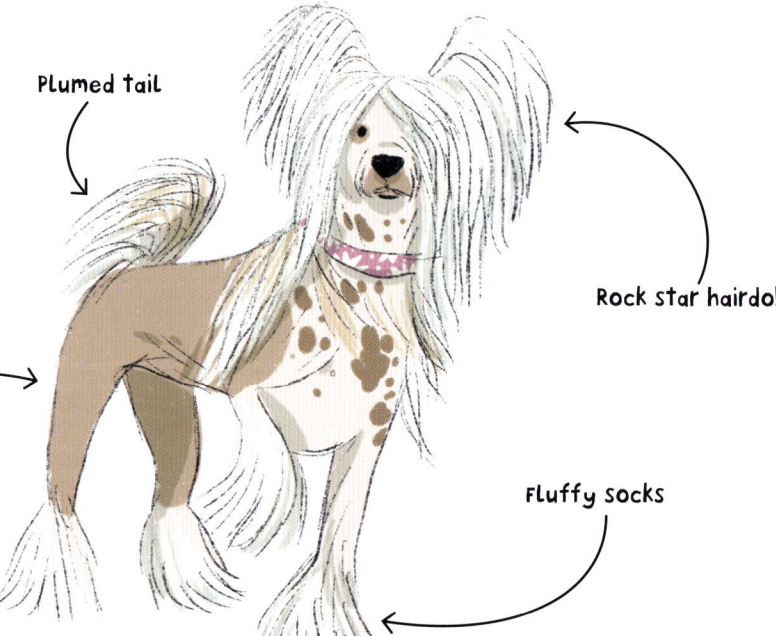

Plumed tail

Rock star hairdo!

Fluffy socks

Hairless body

ORIGIN: China
COAT: Mostly hairless with long, silky areas
PERSONALITY: Friendly and social

INTELLIGENCE 🐾🐾🐾
ENERGY LEVEL 🐾🐾🐾
TRAINABILITY 🐾🐾🐾

FUNNIEST HAIR 19

Poodle

The dog best known for its fancy haircuts has to be the poodle! Many owners like to clip and groom their pet's fur into all kinds of different shapes. However, there is much more to poodles than their looks! They are one of the most intelligent dog breeds.

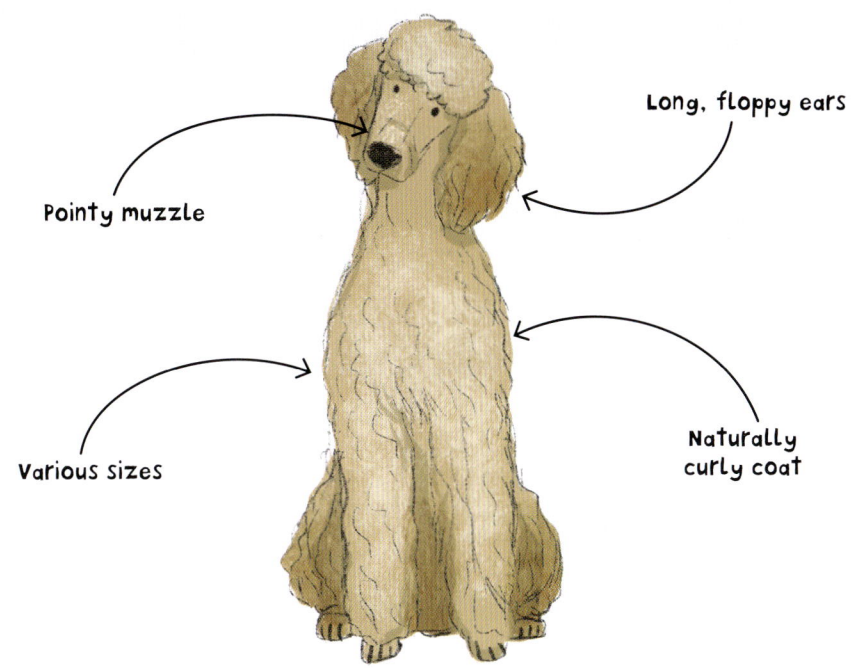

- Pointy muzzle
- Long, floppy ears
- Various sizes
- Naturally curly coat

ORIGIN: Germany
COAT: Medium/long, curly/corded
PERSONALITY: Smart and active

INTELLIGENCE: 🐾🐾🐾🐾
ENERGY LEVEL: 🐾🐾🐾🐾
TRAINABILITY: 🐾🐾🐾🐾🐾

Poodle Haircuts

- continental clip
- corded poodle
- Puppy clip

SPOTTIEST DOG

Dalmatian

This dog is hard to miss, thanks to its iconic spotty coat. Each dalmatian's coat is unique, with a different pattern and number of spots. Puppies are born completely white, with their spots starting to show after a few weeks.

Dalmatians have a history of working as "coach dogs". They would trot alongside carriages to protect the people inside and their horses from robbers. Today, they make loyal family pets.

SPOTTIEST DOG   21

Ears droop forward

Spots, spots, and MORE spots!

Strong body

Thin tail

ORIGIN: Croatia
COAT: Short, smooth
PERSONALITY: Bright but shy

INTELLIGENCE
ENERGY LEVEL
TRAINABILITY

HISTORIC BREEDS

Pharaoh Hound

The pharaoh hound is actually a fairly modern breed, but it bears a very strong resemblance to dogs shown in artwork from ancient Egypt. They are elegant, graceful dogs that can make playful and loving pets.

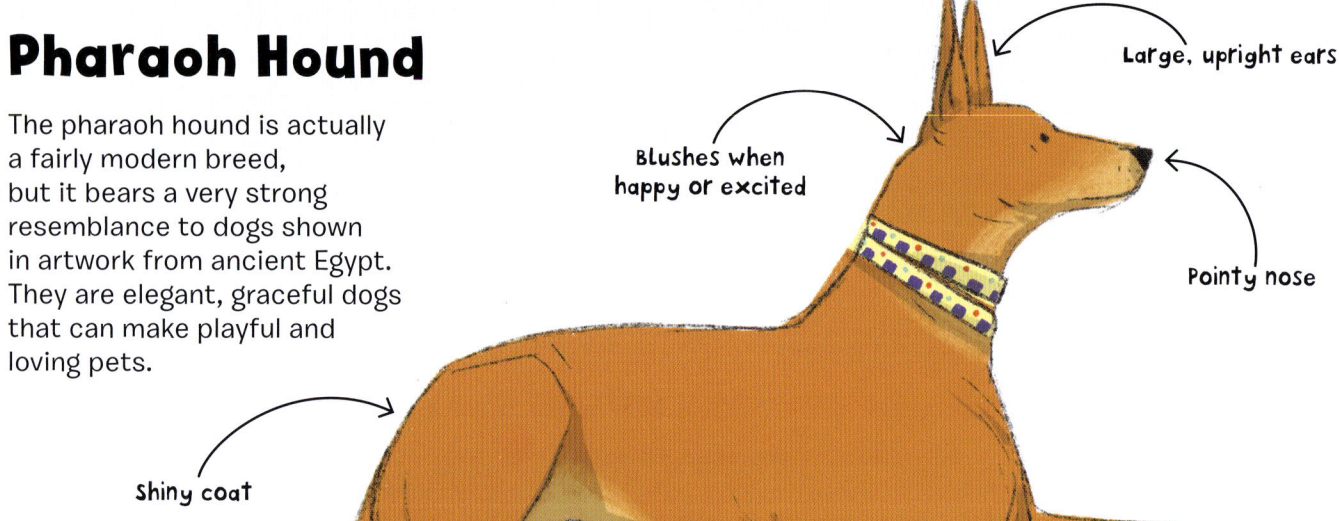

- Large, upright ears
- Blushes when happy or excited
- Pointy nose
- Shiny coat

ORIGIN: Malta
COAT: Short, smooth
PERSONALITY: Sensitive and affectionate

INTELLIGENCE: 🐾🐾🐾🐾
ENERGY LEVEL: 🐾🐾🐾🐾
TRAINABILITY: 🐾🐾🐾

Xoloitzcuintli (Mexican Hairless)

This unusual hairless breed is thought to date back at least 3,500 years! They were important to both ancient Maya and Aztec people, and it was believed that they could help to guide their dead owners into the afterlife.

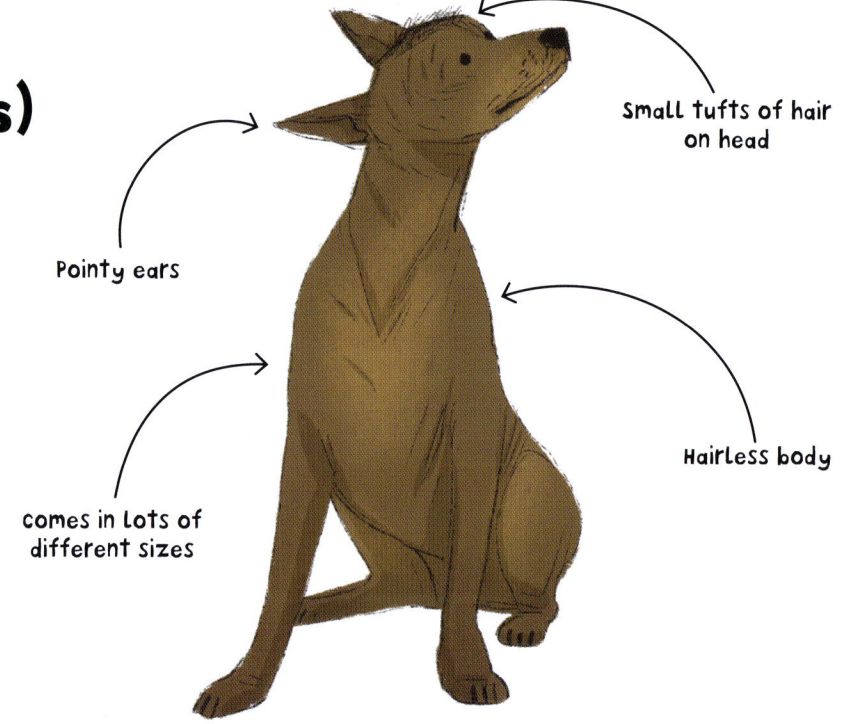

- Small tufts of hair on head
- Pointy ears
- Hairless body
- Comes in lots of different sizes

ORIGIN: Mexico
COAT: Hairless
PERSONALITY: Thoughtful and smart

INTELLIGENCE: 🐾🐾🐾🐾
ENERGY LEVEL: 🐾🐾🐾
TRAINABILITY: 🐾🐾🐾🐾

HISTORIC BREEDS 23

New Guinea Singing Dog

This ancient breed is closely related to the Australian dingo. As their name suggests, they have a special talent for "singing". They have tuneful, yodel-like howls, and sometimes "sing" together, in a chorus. They mostly live semi-wild, so don't make easy pets.

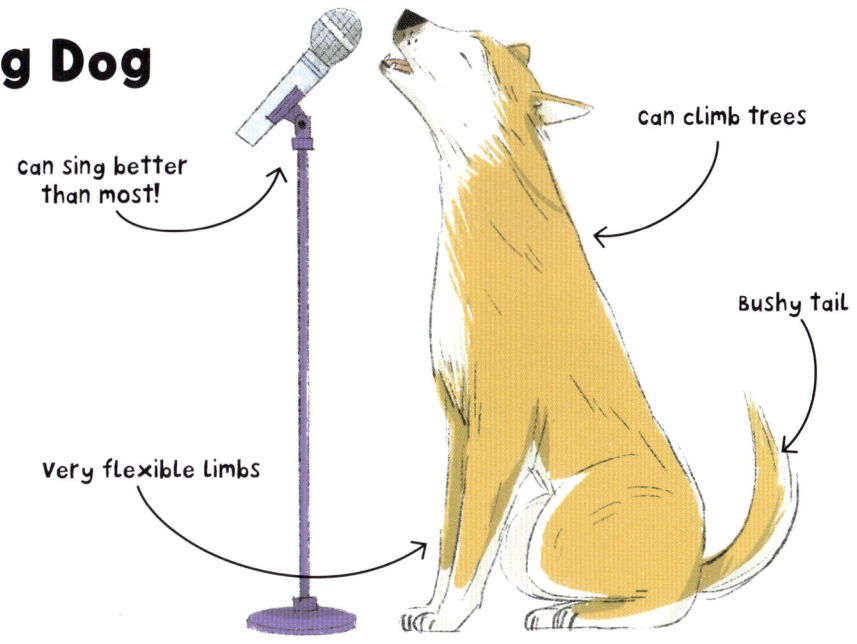

can sing better than most!

can climb trees

Bushy tail

Very flexible limbs

ORIGIN: New Guinea
COAT: Short, thick
PERSONALITY: Smart and Independent

INTELLIGENCE
ENERGY LEVEL
TRAINABILITY

Basenji

The basenji is an ancient breed of African hunting dog. It doesn't bark, but makes yodelling noises, similar to the New Guinea singing dog. Cave paintings of similar-looking dogs have been found in Libya that date back 6,000 years.

curly-wurly tail

wrinkled forehead

Long legs

ORIGIN: Democratic Republic of the Congo
COAT: Short, smooth
PERSONALITY: Smart and Independent

INTELLIGENCE
ENERGY LEVEL
TRAINABILITY

WHAT'S THAT DOG?

Now that you have read all about these unusual dogs, how good are you at identifying them? There are 25 different dogs to figure out. Use the information in the book to help you.

1. What am I?
A. New Guinea Singing Dog
B. Chinese Crested
C. Komondor

2. What am I?
A. Pharaoh Hound
B. Bulldog
C. Bearded Collie

3. What am I?
A. Irish Wolfhound
B. Dachshund
C. Yorkshire Terrier

4. What am I?
A. Xoloitzcuintli
B. Dandie Dinmont Terrier
C. Poodle

5. What am I?
A. Bull Terrier
B. Bichon Frisé
C. Komondor

6. What am I?
A. Borzoi
B. Bulldog
C. Basenji

7. What am I?
A. Bearded Collie
B. Dachshund
C. Pharaoh Hound

8. What am I?
A. Dalmatian
B. New Guinea Singing Dog
C. Chinese Crested

9. What am I?
A. Bedlington Terrier
B. Bull Terrier
C. Bearded Collie

10. What am I?
A. Afghan Hound
B. Dandie Dinmont Terrier
C. Poodle

11. What am I?
A. Dalmatian
B. Dachshund
C. Skye Terrier

12. What am I?
A. Chihuahua
B. Pekingese
C. Komondor

What am I?
A. Keeshond
B. Chinese Crested
C. Bulldog

Answers can be found on page 32.

What am I?
A. Pekingese
B. Yorkshire Terrier
C. Skye Terrier

What am I?
A. Chihuahua
B. Bull Terrier
C. Pharaoh Hound

What am I?
A. Affenpinscher
B. Xoloitzcuintli
C. Poodle

What am I?
A. Keeshond
B. Irish Wolfhound
C. Affenpinscher

What am I?
A. Dachshund
B. Chinese Crested
C. Komondor

What am I?
A. Skye Terrier
B. Afghan Hound
C. Poodle

What am I?
A. Yorkshire Terrier
B. Bulldog
C. Bedlington Terrier

What am I?
A. Bichon Frisé
B. Irish Wolfhound
C. Xoloitzcuintli

What am I?
A. Borzoi
B. Dalmatian
C. Keeshond

What am I?
A. Chow Chow
B. Basenji
C. Borzoi

What am I?
A. Pekingese
B. Basenji
C. Pharaoh Hound

What am I?
A. Poodle
B. Chow Chow
C. Affenpinscher

SPOT THE DOG

There are so many brilliant dogs in the world. You can see them everywhere you go: in towns, parks, and sometimes even at the beach! See which of these are the most popular dogs where you live, make a note of them in a notebook if you do spot them.

Irish Wolfhound · Bulldog · Komondor
Basenji · Yorkshire Terrier · Chinese Crested

Which dogs do you think will be the most and least common in your area? Write your guesses in a notebook and check if you were right. You may be suprised how many you spot, now that you know your breeds!

27

Chihuahua

Borzoi

Skye Terrier

Pekingese

Bearded Collie

Chow Chow

Have you spotted me when you're out-and-about?

Have you seen me before?

Dachshund

Bull Terrier

Affenpinscher

Poodle

Dalmatian

Bichon Frisé

TRAINING AND REWARDS

Trained dogs tend to be well behaved, easier to live with and easier to take out and about.

Training

Dogs are very clever, so you can train them to do lots of things. It's easier to teach dogs good habits when they are young. Correcting an older dog to behave is much harder.

You can also teach dogs tricks and commands. Their ability to follow commands is called **obedience**. The basic commands that most dogs are taught are:

Lie down!

Sit!

Fetch!

Rewards

Rewarding your dog teaches them that they did something right. This is an important part of training.

You can reward your dog by giving them lots of fuss, attention and a tasty treat!

Agility

Agility is a sport where dogs complete an obstacle course as quickly and as accurately as possible. Obstacles include ramps, tunnels, and bars to jump over.

Trainers, called handlers, instruct their dog with voice cues and body signals – there are no toys or treats in sight!

Most owners start training their dogs at home, before taking them to agility classes, with other dogs to practise.

It takes a lot of training to win some of the top international competitions.

GLOSSARY

Adopting – Legally taking on the animal as your own, receiving all responsibility.

Agility (dog sport) – a sport where dogs complete complicated obstacle courses, including objects that they have run through, around, under, or jump over.

Burrows – holes or tunnels dug by animals.

Characteristics – a feature or quality of a person, place, or thing.

Corded – a type of dog coat that forms into long rope-like strands, similar to dreadlocks.

Descendants – people or animals that are related to an individual or group who lived in the past. For example, you are a descendant of your parents and grandparents.

Domesticate – to be tamed or trained to live or work with humans.

Lapdogs – dogs that are small enough to sit on someone's lap and make friendly companions.

Obedience – the ability to follow orders and commands. Obedience in dogs shows that training has been successful.

Rehoming shelter – a place where dogs (or other animals) who were lost, stray, or given up by their owners, are looked after until they can be adopted into a new home.

Show clip – a haircut or style used on dogs that compete in dog shows.

Tsar – a Russian emperor, before 1917.

Underbite (or undershot) – when the lower jaw or teeth stick out in front of the upper jaw or teeth, when the mouth is closed.

Wiry – a type of dog coat that is rough, thick, and bristly.

INDEX

A
affenpinscher 10, 27
Afghan hound 16

B
basenji 23, 26
bearded collie 17, 27
bedlington terrier 18
bichon frisé 14, 27
borzoi 11, 27
bulldog 10, 26
bull terrier 11, 27

C
Chihuahua 9, 27
Chinese crested 18, 26
chow chow 15, 27

D
dachshund 12, 27
Dalmatian 20-21, 27
dandie dinmont terrier 13

H
herding group 7
hound 7, 9, 16, 22, 27

I
Irish wolfhound 9, 26

K
keeshond 14
komondor 16, 26

N
New Guinea singing dog 23
non-sporting breed group 6

O
oldest dog breeds 22-23

P
Pekingese 15, 27
pharaoh hound 22
poodle 19, 27

S
scent hound 7
show clip 18-19, 30
sighthound 7, 16
Skye terrier 13, 27
sporting breed group 6

T
terriers 6, 11, 13, 17, 18-19, 27
toy breed group 7

W
working breed group 6, 17, 20

Y
Yorkshire terrier 17, 26

X
xoloitzcuintli (Mexican hairless) 22

WHAT'S THAT DOG ANSWERS

1 - B. Chinese Crested
2 - A. Pharaoh Hound
3 - A. Irish Wolfhound
4 - B. Dandie Dinmont Terrier
5 - C. Komondor
6 - B. Bulldog
7 - A. Bearded Collie
8 - B. New Guinea Singing Dog
9 - B. Bull Terrier
10 - A. Afghan Hound
11 - C. Skye Terrier
12 - B. Pekingese
13 - A. Keeshond
14 - B. Yorkshire Terrier
15 - A. Chihuahua
16 - B. Xoloitzcuintli
17 - C. Affenpinscher
18 - A. Dachshund
19 - C. Poodle
20 - C. Bedlington Terrier
21 - A. Bichon Frisé
22 - B. Dalmatian
23 - C. Borzoi
24 - B. Basenji
25 - B. Chow Chow

ABOUT THE AUTHOR

Annabel is a writer and artist based in London, UK. Having worked as a bookseller for many years, she now writes children's books focusing on animals and the natural world. Her recent titles include *What Can I See in the Wild?*, *Seasons* and *The Spectacular Lives of Sharks*.

ABOUT THE ILLUSTRATOR

Marina is a talented illustrator of children's books from Ukraine. Her stunning illustrations are inspired by her own childhood, children, nature, magical moments and fairytales.

Picture Credits:
(abbreviations: t=top, b=bottom, m=middle, l=left, r=right)

Alexandra Morrison photo 24bl, 27bm; Ammit Jack 24m, 26tm; Anastasia Cherniavskaia 25bm, 27tm; Aneta Junagerova 24m, 27m; AnotnMaltsev 25m, 27bl; Colin Seddon 29ml; Didkovska Ilona 25tr, 27br; Dulova Olga 25tl, 26m; Everita Pane 24tl, 26tr; Grisha Bruev 25bm, 26ml; Jana Oudova 24tm, 26tl; Jaromir Chalabala 29tl; Kalinina Maria 25tm; Kamil Macniak 29br; Ksenia Raykova 29bl; Lenkadan 24tm; Liliya Kulianionak 25ml, 27bl; Lisjatina 25bl, 27bm; Lourdes Photography 24bm, 27tr; Matyas Rehak 29mr; Natalia fesiun 25br, 27mr; OlgaOucharenko 25mr, 27br; Ratchet 25tm, 27tl; Rodomir Rezny 24tr; Sabine Hagedorn 25t; Speedkings 28mr; T.Den_Team 24br, 27tl; Tara Lynn and Co 24mr; Tikhomirov Sergey 25m; WildStrawberry 24bm; Zuzule 24tl, 26mr.

Every effort has been made to trace the copyright holders, and we apologise in advance for any unintentional omissions. We would be pleased to insert the appropriate acknowledgements in any subsequent edition of this publication.